WREATH MAKING BASICS

MORE THAN 80 WREATH IDEAS

DAWN CUSICK

A Sterling/Lark Book
Sterling Publishing Co., Inc.   New York

Design: Dawn Cusick
Production: Elaine Thompson, Dawn Cusick
Illustrations: Crystal Coates Allen
Photography: Evan Bracken, Martin Fox
Cover Design: Chris Colando

Library of Congress Cataloging-in-Publication Data
Cusick, Dawn.
  Wreath making basics : more than 80 wreath ideas / Dawn Cusick.
    p. cm.
  "A Sterling/Lark book."
  Includes bibliographical references and index.
  ISBN 0-8069-0279-5
  1. Wreaths. I. Title.
TT899.75.C86   1993
745.92—dc20   92–41411
                                    CIP

10 9 8 7 6 5 4 3 2

A Sterling/Lark Book

Produced by Altamont Press, Inc.
50 College Street, Asheville, NC 28801 USA

Published in 1993 by Sterling Publishing Co., Inc.
387 Park Avenue South, New York, NY 10016 USA

Copyright 1993, Altamont Press

Distributed in Canada by Sterling Publishing
  c/o Canadian Manda Group, P.O. Box 920, Station U,
  Toronto, Ontario, Canada M8Z 5P9
Distributed in the United Kingdom by Cassell PLC
  Villiers House, 41/47 Strand, London WC2N 5JE, England
Distributed in Australia by Capricorn Link Ltd., P.O. Box 665
  Lane Cove, NSW 2066

Some of the photographs in this book have been reprinted from the following
books with permission from the publisher, Sterling Publishing Co., Inc., New
York: *The Wreath Book* by Rob Pulleyn; *Wreaths 'Round the Year* by Dawn Cusick
and Rob Pulleyn; and *Herbal Wreaths* by Carol Taylor; *Christmas Naturals* by
Carol Taylor; and *A Scented Christmas* by Dawn Cusick.

Printed in Hong Kong by Oceanic Printing

ISBN 0-8069-0279-5

Julianne Bronder is a wholesale designer in Alsip, Illinois. She studied at the American Floral Art School in Chicago and enjoys teaching, consulting, and creating design show presentations. (Pages 16, 25, 47, 61, 73, 78, 84, 86, 92, and 95.)

Fred Tyson Gaylor taught art in the public school system for ten years before changing careers to showroom and movie set design. He is currently a product designer for Hanfords, Inc., a wholesale holiday accessory company in Charlotte, North Carolina. (Pages 11, 12, 15, 55, 57, 60, 67, 75, 79, and 89.)

Cynthia Gillooly owns The Golden Cricket, a floral design studio in Asheville, North Carolina. She enjoys creating innovative designs with natural materials. (Pages 9, 14, 22, 27, 28, 30, 31, 34, 45, 48, 49, 54, 56, 59, 63, 66, 68, 76, 80, 81, 91, and 94.)

Nancy McCauley died in 1991 of heart disease. She is survived by her husband Lowell, three children, and nine grandchildren. Nancy used traditional drying and dyeing techniques to make all of her dried flower and herb crafts. We miss her very much. (Pages 3, 17, 23, 36, 41, 51, and 58)

Sandy Mush Herb Nursery is the full-time passion of the Jayne family. They are located in Leicester, North Carolina, where they grow an extensive variety of herbs that they sell through mail-order catalogs. (Pages 32, 39, 52, 53, 79, and 87.)

Also thanks to . . .
Nora Blose (pages 13, and 19-21), Corinne Erb (pages 50, 70, and 83), Janet Frye (pages 62 and 93), Aubrey Gibson and Michael Staley (pages 24 and 26), Linda Love (page 46), Gail Martin (page 85), Jamie McCall (page 80), Kit Meckly (page 90), Alyce Nadeau (pages 82 and 88), Rob Pulleyn (page 76), Beth Stickle (back cover), Sylvia Tippitt (page 71), Dawn Wade (page 72), and Diane Weaver (page 29 and front cover).

In some respects, a book on the basics of making wreaths seems unnecessary. The craft is so simple: Just attach some pretty materials to a base and *voila!* you have a wreath. The only complicated part of learning to make wreaths is becoming aware of all the choices you have.

What kind of base to use? Straw, foam, wire, moss, or one of the new inventions? What kinds of materials to use? Fresh, dried, paper, or silk? What kind of bow? Paper, cotton, cellophane, velvet, or wired? How will the materials be attached? A glue gun, floral wire, floral picks? What colors to choose? Should they blend or contrast? What kind of mood will the wreath evoke? Country, modern, energetic, or sophisticated? How will the wreath be displayed? On the wall, outdoors, or on a table as a centerpiece? What shape will the wreath be? Round, oval, heart, or square?

This book will help make those questions a lot simpler. Your answers will be educated ones, and your results will be lovely. If you're making a holiday wreath that will spend much of the year packed away in the attic, for instance, you will know to choose a bow made from paper or wire ribbon because it can easily be re-shaped. If you're making a wreath to hang on a living room wall that receives sunshine or on your front door, you'll know which materials won't fade in the sun. If you want to leave a portion of your base left undecorated, you'll know which bases to choose for the best effect.

What will you do after you've learned the basics? Make wreaths, of course. Lots and lots of wreaths. Wreaths for every holiday, for every occasion; wreaths for friends, relatives, and fund-raisers; and maybe even wreaths for that small business you've always dreamed of owning. And when you think you've run out of new design ideas, just thumb through some of the beautiful wreath books listed in the bibliography on page 96 for inspiration.

Enjoy!

There's no getting around it — every wreath must begin with a base. The type, style, size, shape, and cost of your wreath's base, though, is completely up to you. The straw, moss, and vine bases favored by traditional wreath makers are still available, but so are a range of creative options such as foam bases with mirrored centers, bases covered with grated cinnamon, bases made with wet foam to lengthen the life span of fresh flowers, and much, much more. This wide variety of base materials (with corresponding

varieties in sizes, price ranges, and technical considerations) makes it a good idea to have a visual idea of the type of wreath you'd like to make before you choose a base. The pages that *follow explain many of the ben-

efits, drawbacks, attachment methods, and design strengths relevant to each type of base.

Foam bases are comparatively inexpensive and available in more varieties of thickness, size, and shape than any other type of wreath base. You can find them as

small as 2 inches (5 cm) in diameter, in narrow heart shapes, and even large ovals. The biggest drawback to foam bases is they can really distract from the beauty of a finished wreath if small holes or gaps are visible. Other wreath makers dislike the foam surface for glue adhesion: some craft glues just peel off while some hot glues are hot enough to melt the foam. These two problems, though, can be easily solved by covering the foam surface before you begin working.

The two most popular materials to cover foam bases are moss and ribbon. Spanish, sheet, and other varieties of moss can be folded around the base and secured in place as needed with floral pins. The smaller your wreath base, though, the more difficulty you'll have using the floral pins. Ribbon some-

times makes a better choice because you can match the ribbon's color to the wreath's materials. With very small bases, choose a narrower ribbon and secure it to the foam with sewing pins. If portions of the base will not show in the finished base, you can substitute strips of cotton

fabric for the ribbon.

Many of the larger foam bases are available with a thick wire ring that's been molded with the foam to add strength when you're working with heavy materials. Wire-reinforced foam bases should also be used when the materials will not be evenly arranged around the base to prevent the stress of the unequal weight distribution from cracking the foam.

Single-wire bases are the ideal choice when working with light-weight materials such as pussy willow, pepperberries, and dried flowers because the finished wreath will be thin and delicate, creating a pleasant design reiteration of the materials. Be sure you consider where you'll be displaying this type of wreath before making it. The wreath will look wonderful in a small room, centered over a light piece of furniture, but will look out of place in

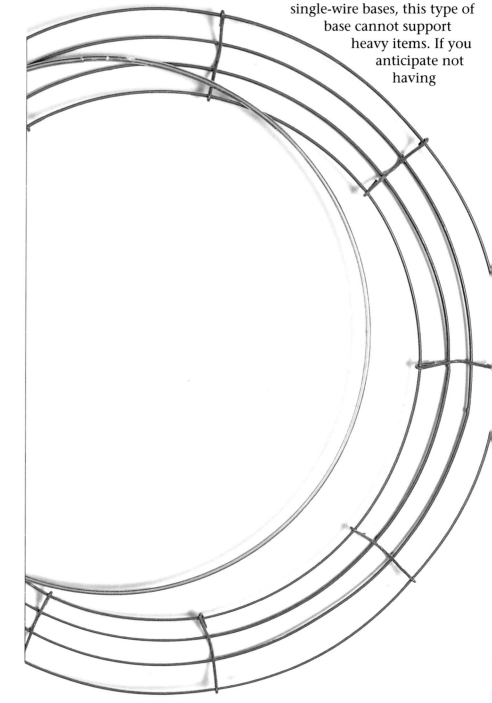

a very large room or centered over a large focal point such as a rock fireplace. Single-wire wreath bases are not a good choice when you're working with larger items because there just isn't enough surface area to glue things onto, and it's impossible to arrange the materials at interesting angles without creating lots of unattractive gaps. Single-wire wreath bases will not accommodate a lot of weight.

Double-wire wreath bases are also available, allowing you to create a flat, wide surface by wrapping brown shipping paper or a colorful paper ribbon around the two wire rings. This kind of base creates less of a three-dimensional wreath, so this is a good base choice if you're making a wreath to display in the narrow space between a storm door and an outside door. The flat surface created by covering the rings with paper also enables you to work with large, delicate materials such as dried peppers that would break if you tried to fold them around the curves of a foam, straw, or vine base. Like single-wire bases, this type of base cannot support heavy items. If you anticipate not having enough materials to densely cover the base, be sure to choose the paper or ribbon in a color compatible with the materials so the spaces won't be too obvious in the finished wreath.

Wire wreath bases are also available with multiple rings of wire that have been arranged at different depths to create a trench that can be filled with moss, pine needles, or fragrant herbs such as sweet Annie or mint. These custom bases are ideal if you have only a few dried flowers to work with but you want a round, full-shaped wreath. If you plan to display the wreath on a table, just arrange the materials compactly inside the trench, taking care to conceal the outer wire ring; if the finished wreath will be hung on a wall, you will need to secure the materials inside the trench by loosely wrapping monofilament or thin-gauge floral wire around the materials and the base. Single leaves or flower blooms can then be hot-glued on top of the natural materials or dabbed with craft glue and inserted into the base material.

Straw wreath bases have long been the first choice among traditional wreath makers, perhaps because it's difficult to top the lush fullness of a straw base that's been decorated with dried flowers. Not everyone has access to enough dried flowers to cover the full surface area of a straw base, though, and buying the dried flowers in bulk from a craft store can get pricey. Straw bases also do not come in the same variety of sizes as other bases because the straw is so thick that the center hole begins to fill in as the diameter of the base decreases.

To prevent the stems of dried flowers and herbs from breaking when they're inserted into a straw

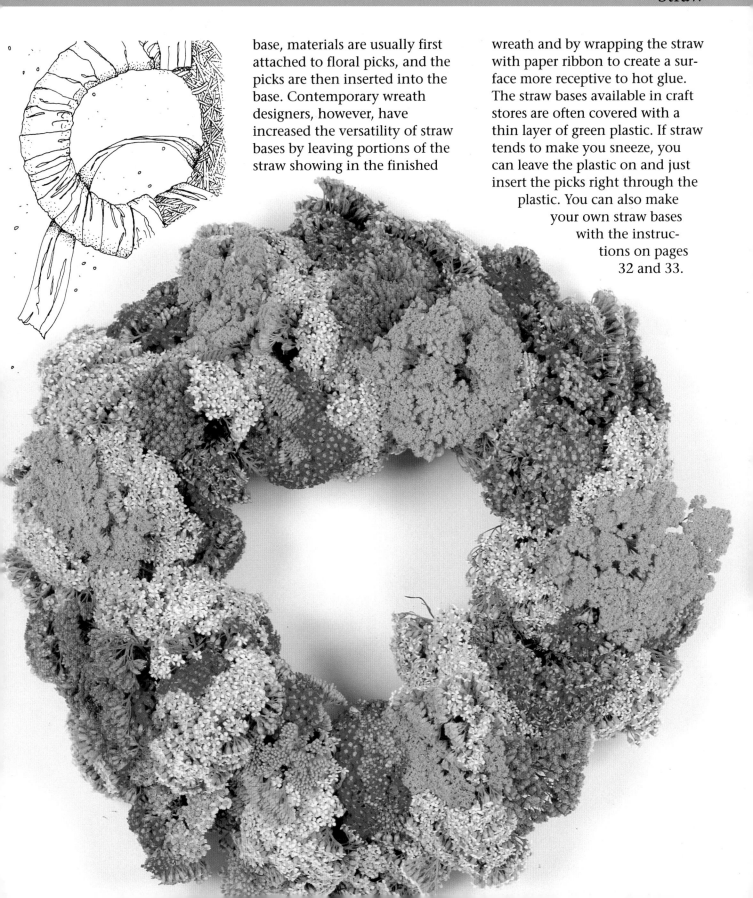

base, materials are usually first attached to floral picks, and the picks are then inserted into the base. Contemporary wreath designers, however, have increased the versatility of straw bases by leaving portions of the straw showing in the finished wreath and by wrapping the straw with paper ribbon to create a surface more receptive to hot glue. The straw bases available in craft stores are often covered with a thin layer of green plastic. If straw tends to make you sneeze, you can leave the plastic on and just insert the picks right through the plastic. You can also make your own straw bases with the instructions on pages 32 and 33.

Vine bases are an all-around good choice for a multitude of reasons. The natural vine is so attractive that designers often leave large portions of the base uncovered, so you need far fewer materials to make a vine wreath. Vine bases also accommodate a wide range of styles. With simple everlastings and a polka dot bow, the wreath looks country; add some dried fruit, some exotic flowers, and the wreath will work in even the most formal of homes. When shopping for vine bases, look for firm, nicely colored vine with a multitude of curly tendrils.

Vine bases are also easy to make if you have access to vine (see pages 34 and 35). Wreaths displayed over large walls or fire-places are often made from vine bases because even a 6-foot-diameter (1.8 m) vine base is fairly light-

weight. If you're custom-making a vine base for a specific location, check to be sure the base is proportionate to the display location and add more rows of vine to increase the size if necessary.

To attach materials to a vine base, hot-gluing and wiring are the methods of choice. If you're working with multiple stems of dried flowers or herbs, they can be attached to a floral pick (see page 38) and then inserted at an angle into the vines after a dab of hot glue has been added to the end of the pick. Fresh and silk fruits and vegetables, which seem to go so well with vine bases, can be wired (see pages 42 and 43) to the base and then reinforced with a dab of hot glue if necessary. Before you actually attach your materials to the base, though, be sure to hold them against the vines to see if you like the effect—dark-colored materials sometimes blend in too much to be appreciated, whereas bright-colored materials contrast very well.

Moss bases are well-liked for several reasons. First, they provide a good adhesion surface for glue as well as being receptive to floral picks and single stems of flowers or greenery. Second, their natural look allows wreath makers to decorate the top, bottom, or just one side of the base and leave the remaining surface area bare for an attractive alternative to the traditional-looking wreath. You can pur-

chase several sizes of moss bases in craft supply stores or make them yourself from scratch. (See pages 36 and 37 for directions.) You can also cover a foam or straw base with moss to create a surface that's more receptive to hot glue. To cover a base with moss, just

arrange the moss around the top and sides, and then secure in place with floral pins or with loose wraps of monofilament or thin-gauge floral wire.

Several varieties of mosses are sold in small packages in craft stores. If you opt to pick your own moss, however, be sure to find out which varieties, if any, are endangered in your area. Even if none are endangered, it's still a good idea to harvest only a little moss from each area so you don't damage the ecosystem.

'Silver King' and 'Silver Queen' artemisias make a wonderful base material for wreaths. The feathery, silver foliage of this perennial herb makes it an ideal background for dried flower and herb wreaths. Pastels seem to blend right in to the delicate gray of the artemisia, while bright colors seem brighter with the contrast. The fresh, clean scent is a nice bonus.

You can order these artemisias in dried bunches from herb farms or grow them yourself. Like most herbs, the plants don't mind dry soil and hot sun, and they re-seed themselves so if you buy one plant this year you will have ten plants next year.

To make dried artemisia into a wreath base, hold it against a single-wire ring or place it in a trench wire base and secure by wrapping several times with monofilament or thin-gauge floral wire. Single dried flower blooms can then be hot-glued onto the artemisia, while stems of dried flowers and foliage can be dabbed with hot glue and inserted deep into the artemisia.

Sweet Annie, actually a type of artemisia, has been culti-vated for its fragrance for centuries. A hardy perennial, sweet Annie likes sun and doesn't mind dry soil, so you may wish to grow it yourself rather than purchase it from an herb farm or craft supply store. Harvest the plant any time after it has bloomed, and hang it upside down to dry in bunches of four to six stems.

Few people find Sweet Annie's pungent yet clean frgrance objectionable, and the fragrance can be released when-

ever you like by simply rolling a few of the seeds between your fingers. The delicate look of the small blooms and foliage makes this the perfect background material for dried flowers in pastel colors, such as pink larkspur, miniature carnations, and miniature roses.

To make dried sweet Annie into a wreath base, hold several dried stems against a single-wire ring or place it in a trench wire base and secure by wrapping several times with monofilament or thin-gauge floral wire. Single dried flower blooms can then be hot-glued into the sweet Annie, while the stems of dried flowers and foliage can be dabbed with hot glue and inserted deep into the sweet Annie.

Fragrant culinary herbs make the perfect base for kitchen wreaths. If you're new to growing herbs, you may find the idea of making wreath bases from fresh-cut plants just scandalous. With most perennial herbs, though, you'll have lots of extra plants to spare after the first year of growth, and by the third year you'll be making culinary wreaths for everyone on your gift list.

Bay, oregano, and sage make lovely backgrounds for whole heads of garlic or dried red peppers. If you live in a climate that's warm year 'round, you can trim a bay tree for leaves. If you live in an area where bay isn't winter-hardy (and thus is more difficult and expensive to come by), you can order a pre-made bay base from an herb farm.

Wreath makers value bee balm for its beautiful, fragrant blooms ranging in color from pastel pink and lavender to a brilliant magenta. Like other members of the mint family, this innocent-looking perennial throws root runners and multiplies with great speed. While you may be familiar only with peppermint or spearmint,

there's another whole world of mints out there. Ginger mint, orange mint, grapefruit mint, pineapple mint, apple mint, and chocolate mint are just a few. The foliage usually dries to a nice dark green, and the fragrances remain subtle for years to come.

To make dried bay or sage leaves into a wreath base, attach 3-inch stems of bay to floral picks (see page 38) and insert the picks into a

straw base. For a thinner base, hold the stems against a single-wire ring and secure them by wrapping several times with floral wire. Continue positioning additional stems to overlap the stems of the previous leaves until the entire wire ring is covered.

To make dried oregano, bee balm, or mint into a wreath base, hold several stems against a single-wire ring or place it in a trench wire base and secure with several wraps of monofilament or thin-gauge floral wire. Single herb blooms and/or culinary items can then be hot-glued onto the oregano, while stems of dried herbs and foliage can be dabbed with hot-glue and inserted deep into the oregano.

Surprisingly enough, wreath bases can be crafted into gardens for many living plants such as succulents. A few garden shops and mail-order houses carry these types of bases pre-made, but you can make your own at home with not too much effort. To make the base you will need fine chicken wire, a heavy-duty stapler, moss, potting soil, wire cutters, plywood, and several cooperative plants.

First, trace the circle shape of a large straw or vine wreath base onto a piece of plywood and cut out the doughnut center and the outer edges. Then mold the chicken wire over the top of the wood base and staple it to the back side. Soak the moss in water and then pack it with equal amounts of potting soil into the chicken wire.

Last, plant an assortment of succulents around the wreath. To increase visual appeal,

small mushrooms and fungi can be hot-glued to the moss.

Keep the wreath sitting flat for a few weeks so the plants can take root. The wreath can be hung indoors, although you may want to take it down when you water it every few days.

This clever wreath base combines two of crafting's favorite mainstays — wreaths and baskets — into a single base that lends itself to all kinds of creative possibilities. The basket can be filled with potted plants, Christmas orna-

ments, decorative soaps, or fragrant sachets. It can also be used for the mundane and functional, such as a place to stash telephone messages or magazines. If you're making a flower wreath, prepare the basket by filling it with moss or moss-covered foam. Stems of dried, silk, or paper flowers can then be inserted directly into the foam, while single blooms can be hot-glued directly to the moss.

A very simple idea — mounting a piece of glass against the back of a foam base — creates a base with potential for creating very elegant, formal wreaths that make ideal decorations for wedding and anniversary celebrations. You can attach the mirror to the back of a base yourself with hot glue, or purchase the base pre-assembled from most larger craft stores.

Materials are inserted into or hot-glued to the foam base just as you would any other foam base. The reflections add an intriguing multi-dimensional appeal, which can be increased by using brightly colored materials. These wreaths make the perfect decorations for celebration parties.

A simple foam base covered with cinnamon emits a rich fragrance even after it's been decorated, and the fragrance can be rejuvenated as needed with a few drops of cinnamon-scented essential oil.

Materials can be picked, wired, or hot-glued to the cinnamon-covered base just as you would any other foam base, but it makes sense to choose a design that leaves a portion of the base showing, as the wreath shown here does.

Although you could make an afternoon project of crushing cinnamon sticks and gluing the powder to a foam base, it's a lot easier to purchase the wreath pre-covered and spend your energy making the wreath instead.

Wreaths are well known for their round shape, which was probably originally chosen for its symbolic meaning of fullness, completeness, and coming together. But perhaps because the circle shape is so entrenched in history, making wreaths with other shapes is downright exciting, a chance to throw caution to the wind and break tradition, even for the most conservative of us.

The bases for shapes such as ovals and hearts can be purchased in craft supply stores, while others will need to be made at home with some imagination and a cooperative material such as fresh-cut vine, foam, or floral wire.

The base for the unusual wreath shown below was made by drawing the pattern on a piece of paper, gluing the paper to a piece of foam, and then cutting out the shape with a serrated knife. The foam was then sculpted with the knife to create various levels, and then decorated by hot-gluing individual flowers and leaves in place.

The base for the square-shaped wreath shown at right was made from a piece of foam core cut into a square. Square bases can also be made by shaping several strands of fresh-cut vine into a square and then hot-gluing small twigs into the vine to fill out the shape.

Unique wreath shapes can
also be made by securing several
purchased wire or foam bases
together with duct tape or heavy-
gauge floral wire, or by unfolding
coat hangers and reshaping them
in interlocking positions. If you
undertake a wreath like this one

made from three small foam bases, though, you'll need to add extra details to make them look right as a whole. The designer of this wreath, for example, tied the look together with streamers from a French ribbon bow and extra flower accents at the top of the center wreath.

To make a straw base you will need several handfuls of straw, an unfolded coat hanger or length of heavy-gauge wire, and a spool of thin-gauge floral wire or monofilament.

First, shape the coat hanger or heavy-gauge wire into a circle that's at least 12 inches (30 cm) in diameter. Next, gather a small handful of straw and position it against the wire ring. Secure the straw to the wire circle by wrapping the wire or monofilament several times around the straw and the wire circle in 1-1/2- to 2-inch (4 to 5 cm) intervals.

Continue adding new handfuls of straw to the wire circle as described above until the entire base is covered. Wrap the wire around the straw several times in the same place and trim it with wire cutters. The straw base can now be shaped into a better look-ing circle if desired.

To make a vine wreath base you will need six to eight lengths of fresh-cut vine. If fresh-cut vines are not available, you can soak older vines in a tub of warm water until they soften, which may take several hours or several days. When choosing vines, look for firm, well-shaped lengths

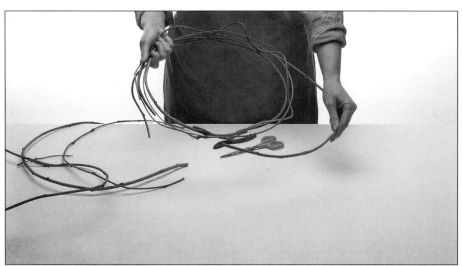

with lots of tendrils and no weak spots from insect damage.

After you've chosen your vines, curve four to six of them around to form a circle, allowing an overlap of about 2 inches (5 cm). Then wrap one or two longer vines around the circle to hold the first vines in place.

Moss bases can be made in several ways. To make a moss base from scratch, you will need several large handfuls of Spanish moss, an unfolded coat hanger or length of heavy-gauge wire, and a spool of medium-gauge wire or monofilament. First, shape the coat hanger or heavy-gauge wire into a circle. Next, hold a large handful of moss against the wire circle and secure the moss in place by wrapping several times with the spool wire or monofilament in 1-1/2- to 2-inch (4 to 5 cm) intervals. Continue adding handfuls of moss to

the wire circle until the entire base is formed. If you're happy with the thickness of your base, you can stop here; or you can increase the surface area of the wreath base by adding more layers of moss.

Moss bases can also be created with a couple of large handfuls of moss, a straw or foam base, and several floral pins. Just curve the moss around the base and secure in place as needed with floral pins. Fresh-picked mosses should be secured in place while they're still damp to prevent breakage. Note: See page 17 for tips on harvesting fresh moss.

Floral Picks

These wonderful gadgets are actually small wooden picks with short lengths of fine-gauge wire attached. They are used to secure stems of flowers or foliage that are too weak to insert directly into a foam or straw base. The end of the pick is pre-cut at an angle to make perforation into the base easier. Floral picks can also be used as a time-saving device: Instead of picking one stem into a base at a time, you

can attach small bouquets of materials to a single pick. There's no set rule about how many stems should be in each bouquet. Three to five is a good guideline, but some materials may have such thin stems that you can pick eight or nine together, while others may be so thick that you'll have difficulty attaching two stems to a floral pick.

To use a floral pick, position the pick against the stem(s) so the pick extends about 1 inch (2-1/2 cm) below the stems. Wrap the wire around the stems twice in the same place, then wrap and spiral the wire down around the stems and the pick to bind them together. Trim the stems where the wire ends. If the stems are

especially fragile, you can add strength by wrapping the picked stems with floral tape.

Floral picks work best with compact straw bases. They will also work with foam bases if the foam is very dense and you don't try to insert the picks too close

together. Floral picks can be used with vine bases if the vines are woven closely together; if the vine weave is loose, you may need to add a dab of hot glue to the tip of each pick before inserting it into the vine.

Craft Picks

Craft picks are floral picks without the wire, and they're used primarily to attach materials

such as fresh fruits and vegetables to a craft base. The sharp end of the pick easily perforates the fruit or vegetable, and then the protruding end is hot-glued into a foam, straw, or vine base.

Floral Pins
These U-shaped pieces of wire look and work like old-fashioned hairpins. Purchase the pins in a color (green and silver are avail-

able) that will blend in with your materials. To use a floral pin, simply position the materials you're attaching against a straw, foam, or moss base, position the pin with its prongs on either side of the material, and press the pin into the base at an angle.

Floral Tape
Floral tape comes in several shades of brown and green that are compatible with natural materials. Floral tape is most often used to add strength to a floral pick that's holding multiple delicate stems. The only trick to success with floral tape is to stretch it gently as you're working with it to increase its adhesive quality.

Glue Guns

Although you could make lots of very nice wreaths without ever using a glue gun, you will miss out on a lot of creative fun if you try to work without one. Glue guns enable you to attach virtually anything to a wreath base in just seconds. So if you're spread out on your kitchen table this winter making a Christmas wreath and you run out of (or get tired of) holly berries, your glue gun enables you to send a roving eye

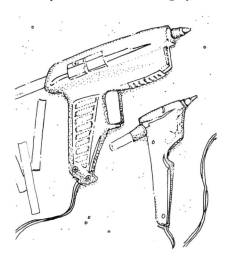

around the house for alternatives. There's no telling what could end up in your wreath: Christmas tree ornaments, garlic bulbs, apples, kids' toys, pomegranates…with a glue gun, anything's possible.

To use a glue gun, you simply plug it in, insert a glue stick, and wait a few minutes until the gun heats up enough to melt the glue. Then you aim the gun where you want the glue and pull the trigger. It's that simple. The only challenging part is avoiding the painful burns the hot glue can cause.

Glue guns come in two varieties (hot melt and low melt), and in two sizes (standard and mini). If you're new to wreath making and don't want to invest a lot of money, the mini glue gun will work just fine for about half to a quarter of the cost of the standard sizes. The benefits of the bigger glue guns include less time spent re-loading glue sticks and the availability of low-melt models whose glue melts at a temperature low enough to not cause severe burns. (The only negative to low melt glue guns is that they require special glue sticks that tend to be more expensive than regular glue sticks.)

Working Tips

• Spread out a protective layer of newspaper over your work area

while your glue gun heats up. If your glue gun does not have a stand, find a glass plate or other non-flammable item to rest it on.

• Don't worry about the strands of dried glue that will appear as you work. Just gently pull them off when you've finished making the wreath.

• Play with angles and positions of your materials before you apply the first bit of glue.

• Hold larg-

er items in place for at least a minute to ensure good bonding. Heavy items may need to be wired to the base first and then reinforced with hot glue.

• Keep a bowl of ice cubes near your working area to treat glue burns. If you're in a rush, tend to

be on the clumsy side, or are working at an odd angle, you may want to wear a pair of thin garden gloves while you work.

• Unplug your glue gun whenever you leave its sight.

• If you have children in the house, be sure to store the glue gun in a safe place. You wouldn't want to find the cat's tail hot-glued to the tricycle or an antique vase to the refrigerator door.

Floral wire is one of those inexpensive, invaluable tools every crafter should have around the house. It's available in a variety of different thicknesses (referred to as gauge), in several different colors (brown, green, and silver), and is sold in pre-cut lengths and on spools. Thin and medium gauges of wire tend to be more flexible and thus easier to work with, although the thicker gauges can add some much-needed strength if you're trying to attach an unusually heavy item to a base. Always choose the color that will blend in best with the materials you're working with. Short lengths of floral wire are used to attach single items, such as bows, to wreath bases, whereas wire in spool-form is used to attach small bouquets of dried or artificial flowers to single-wire wreath bases.

Why, you might ask, would you go to the trouble of cutting a length of wire, twisting it around the item, and then twisting it around the base (total elapsed time: 2-1/2 minutes) if you could attach the same item in seconds with a dab of hot glue?

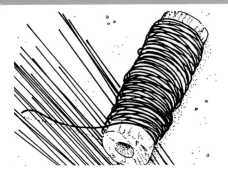 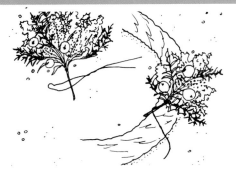 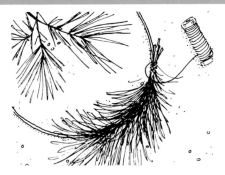

Well, there are several good reasons. With some items you may wish to play with the precise angle and placement on the wreath, and with hot glue there's no time for playing. Other times, you may want to change a bow for a look more appropriate to the season, and if the bow is wired in place this is a very simple procedure: Just untwist the wires of the old bow and wire on the new bow. You may also choose wire as your attachment method when the item is something you cherish, such as a tree ornament that's been in the family for years — and you want to display it in a wreath but don't want it damaged from hot glue.

To wire a single item to a base, first cut a length of wire to approximately 12 inches (30 cm). Examine the item you want to attach to the base for an inconspicuous place to attach the wire. When you're wiring bows, for example, you can slip the wire through the center loop and no one will ever be the wiser.

If an inconspicuous place to attach the wire doesn't exist, you'll need to do some thinking about how you can disguise the wire once the item's on the wreath. With a teddy bear, for example, you can wire it around the neck and then cover the wire with a big bow. With other items,

you may wish to disguise the wire by hot-gluing on small pieces of dried flowers or silk greenery.

Center the wire on the item and twist both ends of the wire together just under the item. Now choose the location on your base where you'd like the item to appear. Hold the item tightly against the base, and twist the wires together again until the tension is tight enough to hold the item in place. If you're not sure of the position, you can leave some slack in the wire while you play with angles. Reinforce heavy items with some hot glue and trim the wires with wire cutters when you've finished.

To attach materials to a wire ring base, first cut the stems of the materials to a consistent length. Four-inch (10 cm) lengths work well with the standard 10- to 12-inch-diameter (25 to 30 cm) wire ring bases; for smaller bases, trim the materials to 2-1/2 or 3 inches (6 to 7 cm) in length; for larger bases, trim the materials to 5 or 6 inches (12 to 15 cm) in length. Arrange the materials into small bouquets of three to five stems per bouquet.

Position the first bouquet against the wire ring base and attach it by wrapping the spool wire around the stems of the materials and the base several times. Do not cut the spool wire.

Position the next bouquet so its flowers or greenery overlap the wired stems of the previous bouquet and secure with several wraps of floral wire. Continue in this way until the entire base is covered. You can decide that your wreath is finished at this point or hot-glue single blooms onto the wired materials.

This method tends to create wreaths that are thinner and more delicate-looking than the traditional picked straw, but this is the ideal type of wreath to showcase the soft beauty of materials like pussy willow and German statice. If you decide you'd like a thicker wreath (or if you notice bare spots), you can hot-glue in additional stems of materials until you're satisfied with the fullness, taking care to position the stems at the same angle as the wired materials.

Floral wire can also be used to make small hanging hooks. To do this, make a half-inch (1-1/4 cm) wide loop in a piece of medium-gauge wire and twist several times. If you're working with a vine base, wire the ends of the loop to the vine and trim the wire. If you're working with a straw or foam base, trim both ends of the wire to half-inch lengths, then embed the ends into the back of the wreath and secure with hot glue.

If you find yourself feeling limited by the surface area of the standard wreath base, you can create three-dimensional effects in just about any shape with floral foam. Purchase the foam in large blocks in craft supply stores and then cut it down to size with a serrated knife. The foam will need to be big enough to accommodate the materials you plan to attach to it but not disproportionate to the size of the wreath base.

After you've cut down the foam, you will need to wire it to the base. Next, disguise the foam by arranging moss over it and then securing the moss in place with floral pins. You can now insert long stems of dried materials through the moss and into the foam, or you can hot-glue materials directly to the moss.

For people who love to garden or who just love the look and

smell of fresh flowers, floral tubes will seem like a marvel of crafting ingenuity. These plastic tubes resemble ordinary test tubes, except their lids have narrow slits in them for inserting flower stems and the base of the tubes have long narrow stems.

The tubes' stems come to a sharp point, enabling you to insert them directly into a foam or straw base. Or, if you'd rather, you can simply hot-glue the tubes to the base, taking care to arrange other materials in the wreath to cover the plastic stems. Floral tubes aren't perfect: It's possible there may be some water leakage, so you should choose your display location with care.

If your design taste is somewhere in between the ardent naturalist and the synthetic superstar, these products will become your mainstay. Natural materials such as vines, seedpods, cones, seashells, and many other things can be jazzed up a bit in just minutes.

Spray paint is now an indispensable tool for many wreath makers. Not too many years ago, if you wanted some spray paint, you went down to your local hardware store and made your choice from eight or nine colors — if you were lucky. Today, you should skip the hardware store and shop for spray paint in a craft supply store. The color range in craft spray paints is magnificent — allowing you to match that pristine peach color on your sofa or the marvelous mauve wallpaper in your guest bedroom.

When it comes time to actually use the paint, keep in mind that more is not always better. If you're adding a blue tinge to a lotus pod, for example, add the color in single, light layers, allowing the paint to dry completely between layers. You'll probably find that the lotus pod, like most other natural materials, will look much better with some of its natural color showing through, instead of completely caked with blue. Also remember that it can be a lot of fun, not to mention create beautiful results, to work with several colors of spray paint.

A branch of canella berries, for example, can be lightly misted with a layer of peach spray paint and then, after the paint has dried, misted again with gold spray paint. Larger items, such as pinecones, can be mentally divided into segments and then sprayed a different

color in each segment, with the colors overlapping in some areas for a more natural look.

Another fun place to use spray paint is on vine wreath bases. Spray the paint onto the bare base in light layers, as you would with smaller items, and try to choose a color that will complement the colors in the wreath's materials or in the bow. If you have access to vine and feel up to the challenge of making your own vine bases, you may want to try your hand at the unusual base shown left. Spray paint five to seven vine lengths, each in a different color. Then, after you've woven them into a base, you have a rainbow effect that's completely custom-designed.

Gilding powder, as the name implies, is a metallic powder that can be used to add a gold glimmer to any number of objects. The powder is usually sold in small containers, and looks like the metallic eye make-up so popular in the '70s. Unlike spray paint, it's usually better to add gilding powder after your wreath is finished, to prevent it from rubbing off in all sorts of places where you do not want a tinge of gold. If, for instance, you rambunctiously hot-glued several rocks onto your wreath and now you're having second thoughts, the effect could easily be softened by just dabbing on a bit of gilding powder. This powder is also a great way to transform ordinary wreath materials into something special for the Christmas holidays or for formal occasions.

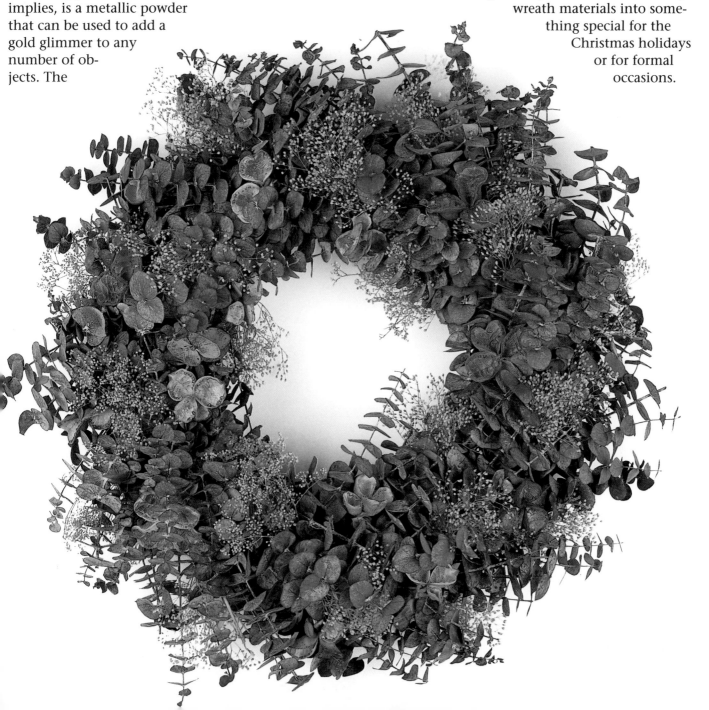

Fresh flowers were chosen by the first wreath makers for their natural beauty, their fragrance, and their symbolic meanings. For these wreath makers, longevity was not a concern: Their wreaths were made for a bride to wear or to adorn a front door on a religious holiday. Today, several creative inventions from the floral industry — floral tubes and wet foam bases — make fresh flowers longer lasting and easier to work with. Floral tubes provide an unobtrusive water source for fresh flowers and can be re-filled as frequently as desired to keep the wreath looking nice. Page 45 provides more details on floral tubes and how to use them.

Wet foam bases are available in larger craft stores and through your florist. Usually a medium to dark green color, these

bases are made from a soft, porous foam that easily absorbs water. Flowers will stay fresh-looking about the same length of time they would in a vase. To work with a wet foam base, simply soak it in water for a few minutes and then insert your flowers directly into the base. Stems should be cut at a sharp angle to make perforation easier and to encourage moisture absorption. If you have materials with weak stems, use a pencil tip to make small holes in the foam before inserting the stems. Wet foam wreaths should be displayed on a table or other flat surface, with a protective layer of paper or plastic underneath to prevent water damage. Once the flowers wilt, simply remove the stems and re-use the base.

Several flowers dry so well that they can actually be hot-glued to a wreath base when they're fresh and then left to dry in place. You need to have some experience with flower drying before you try this, though, because not all flowers dry well, and some flowers shrink so much as they dry that

they'll leave bare spots in the wreath. The following flowers make good choices for beginners because they're easy to dry and shrink very little: globe amaranth, strawflowers, and any kind of statice (annual, German, caspia, etc.).

One nice way to work is to hot-glue the above-mentioned flowers directly to a base and then use floral tubes to add exotic-looking flowers like proteas and iris. Wreaths can also be made from a mixture of fresh and dried materials. The only time you shouldn't mix and match is if you've dried some of your materials in silica gel, because the proximity to the moist, fresh flowers would probably make the silica-dried flowers re-absorb some of the fresh flowers' moisture and wilt.

Centuries ago, each flower and herb had a unique, symbolic mean-

ing, and small gift bouquets were created as messages for loved ones (and ex loved ones!). Many of these flowers and herbs are still cultivated today, allowing wreath makers to create wreaths with symbolic meanings to celebrate special occasions. A birth wreath, for example, can be made from moss (maternal love), honeysuckle (sweetness of disposition), pussy willow (unrealized promise), and bachelor's buttons (single blessedness). A wedding wreath can be made from roses (love), rosemary (remembrance and fidelity), sage (wisdom), chamomile (energy in adversity), and globe amaranth (unfading affection).

Dried flowers and herbs are a mainstay in traditional wreaths. They're almost as beautiful as fresh-cut blooms, but they last for years. You can purchase small bouquets of dried flowers in most craft supply stores, and often in a wider range of color choices than Mother Nature offers because the dried flowers have been soaked in dye baths. If you tend to have trouble with allergies, though, you'll need to sniff before you purchase, since many commercially marketed dried flowers are imported and have been treated with insect repellent. (No sense making a gorgeous wreath only to find out it makes you sneeze!) Also, never display a dried flower wreath on a wall that receives lots of sunlight or the beautiful colors will fade.

A simple, inexpensive alternative to purchasing your dried flowers and herbs is to dry them from your garden. There's nothing mysterious about the process: All flowers and herbs will dry after they've been picked. The problem is, not all of them will look attractive enough to use in a wreath. Many turn brown. Others retain their color yet shrivel up into an unattractive mass. Some keep their shape perfectly but shrink so much during the drying process that you have to dry a lot of extra materials. The paragraphs below explain the basic techniques for harvesting and drying flowers and herbs from your own garden, as well as descriptions of flowers and herbs that almost always dry well. The drying process is complete when the flower or herb feels like a flake of breakfast cereal.

To dry your own flowers, you'll first have to harvest them. Choose a sunny day, after the morning dew has dried and well after a rain shower. Avoid picking materials with damage from insects, and pick a lot more than you anticipate needing to accommodate the natural reduction in size due to shrinkage. Pick flowers in several stages of bloom — from bud form to fully opened — so you can discover which stage holds its color, shape, and size the best.

Most materials can be dried with one of several air-drying techniques. Hanging, the oldest of these techniques, involves grouping several stems of the same flower or herb together, securing their stems together with string or a rubber band, and then hanging them upside down in a dark, dry location. The flowers are hung upside down so the blooms will dry in a more natural position. Another air-drying method, known as screen or rack drying, involves spreading single blooms or leaves on a wire screen that has been arranged so there's ventilation on all sides. Drying times tend to vary, depending on the type of plant and how moist it was when it was harvested. Five to 15 days is an average range.

Flowers can also be dried with desiccants by layering blooms in one of several moisture-absorbing substances, such as borax, kitty litter, sand, or silica gel. Silica gel is the most expensive of these desiccants, but its granules are lighter in weight than the other desiccants and tend not to crush delicate blooms. Check the progress of your blooms every few days to prevent overdrying, and avoid leaving already-dry blooms in a moist area such as the bathroom to prevent the blooms from reabsorbing moisture.

With a new drying method known as microwave drying, the moisture in some varieties of flowers can be removed in just minutes by cooking them with silica gel. Because the moisture in flowers can vary so much from variety to variety and even from day to day, and because the wattages in microwaves vary so much, you will need to allow extra flowers and time for experimenting, but once you perfect the times (and make note of them!) you can dry flowers in minutes for the rest of the summer.

To dry flowers in the microwave, first layer the bottom of a microwave-safe container with a thin layer of silica gel. Arrange the flowers in a single layer so that their sides do not touch and cover them with another thin layer of silica gel. Cook on a medium setting for two-and-a-half minutes and allow a standing time of ten minutes. If your flowers are overdried, start again with fresh materials and reduce the time in 30-second intervals. If the flowers are still not dry, add time in 15-second intervals.

Following is a brief list of some of the most popular flowers and herbs used in wreath making.

Bee Balm should be harvested early in the blooming cycle and can be air-dried on a screen.

Blue Salvia (also known as Indigo Spires) can be air-dried by hanging upside

down in small bundles. The delicate blooms should be handled gently to prevent breakage.

Celosia, both the plumed and crested varieties, holds its color and shape well, and can be air-dried by hanging upside down after the foliage has been removed. Celosia should always be harvested early in the morning to prevent matting.

Dusty Miller is popular for its silvery foliage, which maintains its shape perfectly. The leaves should be spread out on a screen rack to dry and turned frequently.

Roses can be air-dried by hanging stems of just-opened blooms upside down in small bundles. Roses in any stage of bloom can also be dried in a desiccant.

'Silver King' and *'Silver Queen' Artemisias* are dried for their silvery foliage, which makes a nice background material in wreaths. Hang the stems upside down if straight lines are desired, or stand them upright in a bottle if curved lines are desired.

Baby's-Breath dries quickly by hanging upside down in small, loose bunches.

Globe Amaranth's colorful

blooms make wonderful wreath accents, and they air-dry in just a few days on a drying rack.

Larkspur should be harvested for drying when the majority of the flowers on the stalk have opened, and then hung upside down in small bundles to dry. Dried larkspur ranges in color from pale pink, lavender, and cream to deep purple.

Statices are very popular in wreaths because they are so easy to grow and dry. Just hang them upside down for a few days and they're ready to use.

Strawflowers can be dried by spreading the blooms on a rack or hanging the stems upside down in small bundles. They hold their colors wonderfully, and come in all sorts of brilliant shades from purple and red to bright orange and yellow.

Humans have always been fascinated with evergreens and greenery, perhaps because we see them as nature's promise — present even in the coldest of winters — that life will continue. Early civilizations revered evergreens and greenery so much that they made garlands from laurel and olive greenery to celebrate the victories of the first Olympians.

Wreaths made completely from evergreens or greenery form a versatile backdrop for adding seasonal accents. In the spring and summer, tuck water tubes filled with fresh flowers into the foliage and add a festive floral bow. As fall approaches, change the bow, remove the flowers, and wire in some decorative squash. In the winter, replace the bow with a bright red one, replace the squash with some tree ornaments, and tuck in a few sprigs of berries.

Evergreens and greenery also work surprisingly well as filler in wreaths made from knick-knacks, flowers, herbs, and unusual props.

Wreaths made from evergreens and greenery can be assembled in several ways. With strong-stemmed evergreens such as firs, you can simply cut the stems at an angle and in-

sert them directly into a foam or straw base. Materials with more delicate stems can be wired to a wire ring base or attached in small groups to floral picks. Individual leaves can also be arranged around a wreath and hot-glued in place.

Many varieties of evergreens and greenery can be purchased in craft stores and discount marts. These materials have usually been preserved with glycerin, which means they will retain much of their natural color and shape. Materials can be glycerin-preserved at home by filling a small container with three parts water and one part glycerin. Then make several angular cuts in the evergreens' stems and stand them upright in the liquid. As time passes, the evergreens will absorb the glycerin mixture through their stems. The process usually takes about two weeks. Several varieties of leaves also do well with glycerin-preserving, although their fleshier stems may require a higher ratio of glycerin to water. Other materials, such as boxwood, ivy, bay, and mint, can be used fresh in a wreath and then left on the wreath to dry in place.

Berries have been the unfortunate victims of several negative stereotypes among wreath makers. First, it's long been assumed that berries are only for holiday wreaths. Second, crafters often assume that all berries are red. But as the wreaths on these pages demonstrate so beautifully, berries make a wonderful wreath material any time of the year, echoing the round wreath shape with

their small circle clusters and providing a bit of colorful pizazz.

You'll find berries in almost as many colors as flowers. Pepperberries are a common choice because they're often available in larger craft stores and from florists, and because they come in pink

and red varieties. Berries can also be found in foliage, such as 'Silver Dollar' eucalyptus, whose berries are a light green.

Other popular craft berries, such as the canella berry, come in almost every color in the rainbow, thanks to the magic of commercial dyes.

Silk and plastic berries are also good choices, especially if you have young children in the house. Even the most ardent naturalist will be amazed at how nat-

ural these commercial inventions appear, and their fantastic color range is often difficult to resist.

The easiest way to attach berries to a wreath is hot-glue or floral pin them in small bunches. Unless you have a penchant for detail, it's best to save the individual berries for potpourri. (If you insist on adding individual berries to a wreath, however, don't invite burns by using a hot glue gun.)

Renowned for their appearances over the years in holiday wreaths, pinecones, nuts, and seedpods are now used in wreaths for all seasons. Many craft stores offer some very unique selections, although an attentive stroll through almost any wooded area is likely to yield an equally interesting variety. Large flowering trees, such as the magnolia, are also a good source for interesting seed heads and should be checked in the fall. If you choose to collect your own materials, it's probably a good idea to bake them in a 200° F (93° C) oven for 30 minutes to kill any insects.

These natural materials can be used without altering their natural colors or they can be sprayed with your favorite craft paint. Metallics seem to work especially well on these rustic materials, perhaps because of the contrast. For just a touch of jazz, consider dabbing on a little bit of gilding powder to the petals of cones or the edges of nuts and seedpods.

Public perception is often that pinecones, nuts, and seedpods are rough and rustic in nature. Many of them, though, such as minia-

ture hemlock cones and love-in-a-mist, are very small and delicate. Pinecone flowers can be made by placing large cones on

their sides and slicing them in inch-wide (2-1/2 cm) slices.

Cones, seedpods, and nuts can be attached to wreath bases in several ways. To wire a cone to a base, slip a length of medium-gauge floral wire through the bottom petals of the cone and twist the

wires together until tightened. Then wrap the wires around the base and twist again. Extremely heavy cones may need to be reinforced with several dabs of hot glue. Smaller seedpods and heads can be attached to bases with craft picks. Just hot-glue the flat end of the pick to the item and then insert the tapered end into the base. Smaller materials can be simply hot-glued directly to the base.

As a decorative material, moss is often the small touch that ties an entire wreath together. Moss is still one of the last strongholds of nature — it can't be molded from plastic, paper, or silk, as flowers often are. It adds a nice sense of texture to the wreath as well as making the finished wreath look more natural.

Moss also makes wonderful filler material, especially with larger wreaths, when finding enough materials to cover the whole base can be challenging and expensive. Other times, as in the wreath shown on this page, a wreath is made from materials so large that the gaps, however inevitable, and disruptive to the beau-

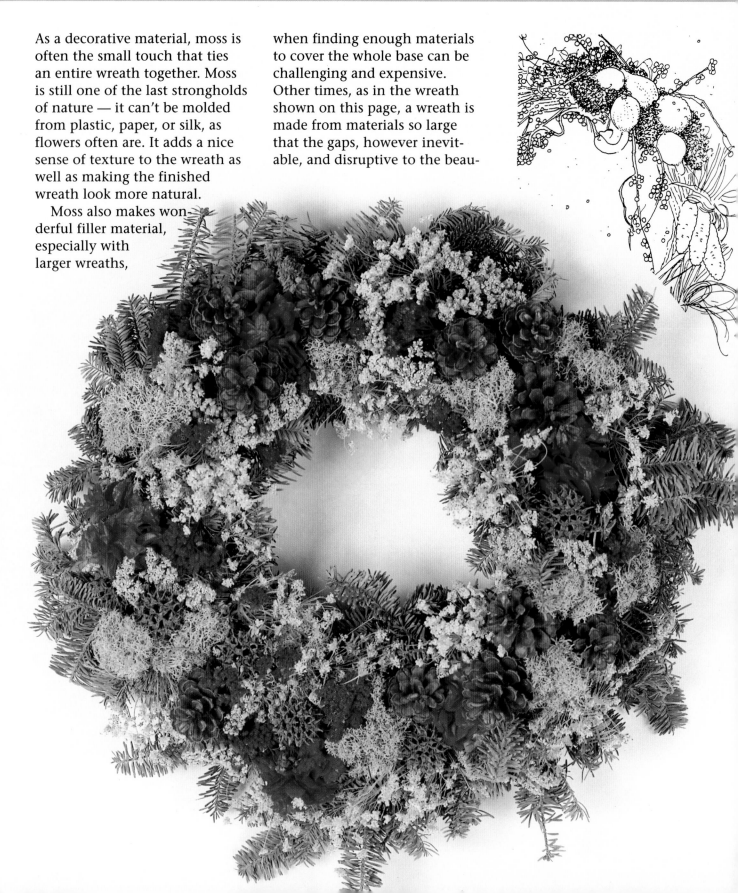

ty of the finished wreath if left unattended. If the gaps are small, you can usually just tuck small clumps of moss into the spaces without using a glue gun.

If the gaps are large, however, you'll probably need to use a glue gun. Be sure to use a pencil or other object to press the moss into the glue to prevent burns.

Several varieties of mosses are sold in small packages in craft stores. Remember, if you opt to pick your own moss, you should find out which varieties, if any, are endangered in your area. Even if none are, it's still a good idea to harvest only a little from each area so you don't damage the ecosystem.

The right bow has the power to transform an average-looking wreath into an extraordinary one, so it makes sense to learn as much as you can about them. The wide range of patterns, colors, and textures available — from polka dots to paisleys, from pastels to brights, from velvet to raffia — lets you control the style of your wreath by your choice of ribbon. A large bow may be the wreath's focal point, while a smaller bow often looks like just another material in the wreath. Once they've been attached to the base, bows can be decorated with dried flowers and other materials, or left as is. Following are brief descriptions of some of the more popular bow materials.

• Satin ribbon's main strength is that it's sold in so many widths that it's easy to make the perfect size bow for your wreath, no matter how big or small it is. Satin ribbon also makes an attractive material to cover foam and straw bases. The ribbon can be too slippery for crafters just learning to tie bows.

• Cotton ribbon makes a good ribbon for beginners because crease marks can be ironed out

with a hot iron so the ribbon can be used again. For admirers of the country look, the lively prints make cotton ribbon a good choice.

• Paper ribbon is sold in long spools and then unrolled before using. It ties easily into simple bows and can be re-shaped if the bow is crushed. Paper ribbon can be reused, so it's a good material for beginners.

• Velvet adds a very formal and tradi-tional look to a wreath, but it's easily crushed and not re-usable if you make a mistake.

• Wired ribbon (also known as French ribbon) is lined with rows of thin-gauge wire on its wrong side so it can be shaped and re-shaped as often as you like.

• Cellophane ribbon adds a hint of holiday glitz to a wreath, and it's an easy material for beginners to work with. The metallic colors may be too bright for some people.

• Raffia adds a natural flair to any wreath. It's easy to work with, and accepts dye well.

• Lace ribbon is the ideal choice for wedding and anniversary wreaths. If it's not stiff enough for the loops to hold their shape, dip it in liquid fabric stiffener before you tie the bow.

If you're working with very contemporary or free-flowing natural materials — such as mushrooms, cooking utensils, etc — a large bow may look out of place. Wired ribbon (also known as French ribbon) can be looped, twisted, and curled around a base to create a free-flowing look. The ribbon's wire enables it to hold these whimsical shapes for a look that's completely natural. Ribbon loops and streamers can be the first or last material secured to the base. If the wreath is for the holidays, you can secure the ribbon to the base every few inches (7 to 10 cm) with a long sewing pin; if the ribbon is to become a permanent part of the wreath, it can be secured with small amounts of hot glue. Paper, cellophane, satin, and cotton ribbons can also be worked around a wreath this way, but the loops and twists will need to be more condensed, and you'll need to secure them to their bases in closer intervals.

If you plan to create an arrangement on one side of the wreath and leave the remaining surface areas undecorated, you can cover a base (usually foam or straw) with ribbon. Start by securing one end of the ribbon to the base with a floral or long sewing pin. Then begin wrapping the ribbon around the base at a slight angle with just enough overlap to prevent the base from showing. Secure the ribbon to the base every few inches (7 to 10 cm) with another pin. It's also a good idea to cover a foam or straw base with ribbon if your materials are so large that there will be large space gaps between them.

Narrow strips of fabric can be substituted for the ribbon if desired.

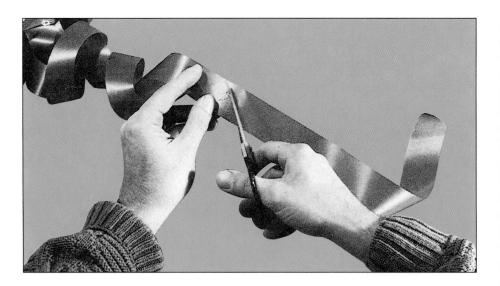

A bow is simply a symmetrical arrangement of ribbon loops that's embellished with streamers. The number and size of the loops and the width of the ribbon determines the look of the finished bow. Learning to tie a bow is a simple process, but you'll need to practice quite a bit before your bows resemble a professional's. The directions that follow explain how to make a bow by first creating a streamer, then constructing two medium-size loops, then two long loops, then two short loops, and finally two more medium-size loops.

First, cut an 8-inch (20 cm) length of ribbon at an angle to form the first two streamers. Crimp the middle of the streamer and hold it tightly between your thumb and index finger. Then make the third streamer by crimping an un-cut length of ribbon about 4 inches (10 cm) in from one end.

Keeping the streamers held tightly, form a medium-size loop (about 3 to 4 inches, 7-1/2 to 10 cm), making sure the right side of the ribbon is facing outward. (Note: A loop consists of two

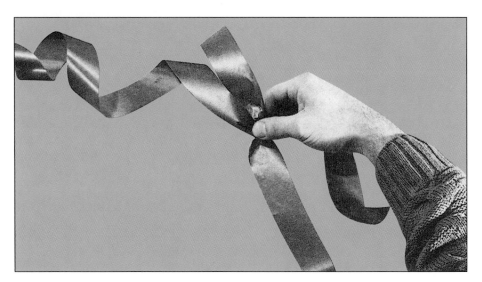

parts, a top loop and a bottom loop.) Now make another medium-size loop, positioning it so it's next to the previous loop and not on top of it. Be careful to keep the center tightly crimped.

Form two larger loops about an inch (2-1/2 cm) longer than the medium-size loops. Now create two smaller loops about an inch smaller than the medium-size loops and position them on top of the large loops. Add two more medium-size loops adjacent to the large loops.

Switch the bow to your other hand, holding tightly to prevent your work from unraveling. Twist a length of thin-gauge floral wire around the streamers and the loops. Trim the un-cut length of ribbon to match the length and angle of the other streamers.

Cover the wire with a short length of ribbon looped around the center and hot-glued in place on the back side of the bow. Fluff and shape the bow by pulling the streamers and rolling your finger around the inside of the loops in the order in which they were added.

In wreath making, natural isn't always better. Sometimes silk, paper, and plastic materials just make more sense. If you plan to display your wreath outdoors, silks and plastics won't be damaged by the elements. If you plan to hang your wreath on an indoor wall that receives direct sunlight, the colors in silk and paper flowers will not fade like those in dried flowers. And,

speaking of color, these materials are always available in popular design colors such as mauve, peach, and country blue. When you shop for silks, papers, and plastics, make your choices carefully: Look for blooms that can arranged in more natural-looking

shapes and for stems lined with thin-gauge wire so they can be curved to suit your wreath base.

Flowers are the most common of these materials, but berries and greenery are quickly gaining in popularity. You may remember plastic leaves as being thick, glossy, and utterly tacky, but manufacturers have responded to the preferences of crafters and improved their products considerably. If you're forced

to use plastic berries because of young children in the house, look for the new varieties that have multiple shades of coloring for a more natural appeal, instead of the glossy look of the past.

Attaching these materials to a base is fast and simple. Long stems of materials like ivy or other greenery can be wrapped around the base and secured in intervals with floral pins or hot glue. Blooms with a strong stem can be inserted directly into a foam or straw base, or dabbed at their ends with hot glue and inserted into a vine base. Wire cutters can be used to clip single blooms and smaller stems of foliage from their main stems, and the blooms can then be arranged around the wreath and hot-glued in place.

While they may look quite ordinary on the grocery market shelves and in your fruit dish at home, fruits and vegetables add an unexplainable burst of excitement to wreaths. Their natural colors, textures, and shapes blend in perfectly with flowers and other natural materials, and you can also make wreaths exclusively from these materials. Fruits and vegetables also make spectacular

table wreaths for centerpieces, and the materials allow for all kinds of design flexibility. Instead of covering a foam base with ribbon, for instance, you can cover it with bright purple radicchio leaves, securing them in place as needed with floral pins.

The only real trick to working successfully with fruits and vegetables is to keep scale in the forefront of your mind as you assemble the wreath. If you're working with a 10-inch (25 cm) base, for example, chances are that an artichoke would look out of place because it is proportionately too big.

Likewise, single grapes would get lost on a 30-inch (75 cm) wreath base, but larger clusters would not.

Two considerations should be taken into account before you decide which method to use to attach your materials. The first consideration is the weight and size of the item. Small, light items such as mushrooms or radishes can be hot-glued in place; medium-weight items such as potatoes and apples can be attached with craft picks; large, lightweight materials such as grape clusters and lettuce leaves can be attached with floral pins; and heavier items such as broccoli and squashes may need a combination of wiring and hot glue to stay in place. The second consideration is whether you want the materials in your finished wreath to be edible, in which case you obviously want to avoid using hot glue.

Keep in mind that the weight of all these fruits and vegetables can add up, making your wreath too heavy to hang unless you've used a wire-reinforced base. Also, remember that you don't have to fill every square inch with fruits and vegetables — just tuck in sprigs of Spanish moss for a totally natural look.

Raiding the kitchen cupboards is a sure way to produce innovative wreaths. Cinnamon sticks, star anise, garlic bulbs, chili peppers, bay leaves nutmeg, allspice berries, cloves, and even small pieces of candy all look nice in wreaths. Arrange a bag of assorted whole nuts around a foam wreath base, hot-glue them in place, dab on a little gilding powder, and you've got a terrific wreath. Dried beans are another versatile wreath

material — you'll need a lot of patience and a steady hand to avoid hot-glue burns, but the terrific designs are more than worth the effort. Bows made from raffia seem to look especially nice on wreaths made from kitchen materials.

If you have an open mind, Mother Nature offers a wonderful assortment of wreath materials. Fungi, lichens, sea shells, feathers, and bee and wasp nests are just a few of the possibilities. Offer a neighborhood child a dollar for a bag of such goodies, and you'll be amazed at the results. These items work equally well as background materials or as accents, so quantity isn't really important. Small, lightweight

materials can be hot-glued in place. Feathers can be inserted by their stems directly into a foam base.

When looking for innovative
wreath materials, it often helps to
search the room where you plan
to hang the wreath. If you're

making a wreath for your sewing
room, for instance, thread spools,
fabric scraps, embroidery floss,
thimbles, and bobbins are all fair
game. For a wreath you plan to
hang over your dressing table, old
jewelry and handkerchiefs can be
borrowed. And for the bathroom,
consider making a wreath from
fragrant bath soaps in assorted
shapes and colors, ac-
cented with a bow
tied from a deco-
rative hand

The next time a birthday rolls around for someone who has virtually everything, consider making a custom wreath with materials from their favorite hobby. A wine connoisseur, for example, would love a wreath like the one below made from wine corks. (Don't worry — many craft stores sell wine corks by the bag, so you won't end up with shelves of un-corked wine.) A chef would enjoy a wreath made from

cooking utensils. (Again, you won't have to spend a lot — just shop garage sales or dime stores for bargains.) The same type of wreath could be made for a gardener, with digging tools, old gloves, and some miniature clay pots.

At Christmas time, a trip to the local discount mart for a box of ornaments and sundry tree trimmings will provide more than enough materials to make lots of wreaths. Or, if you've spent years collecting ornaments for a perfectly coordinated tree, you can just borrow a few ornaments and find some matching ribbon so the tree will match the wreath. Even heirloom ornaments can

be showcased in a wreath; wire
them gently in place or tuck
them into the greenery so they
won't be damaged. Tinsel, garlands, and beads can also be
looped around a wreath base
with stunning results.

Don't be afraid of using larger items in a wreath. Hats, shoes, sunglasses, car parts, old music instruments, sheet music, bells, figurines, children's toys, dolls, and stuffed animals all have potential as wreath materials. These larger items, often referred to as props, can easily establish a theme for a wreath. Because of their size, they are usually attached to the wreath's base with a combination of wire and hot glue. Junk drawers, closets, and garage sales are good sources for these materials.

After you've chosen a prop and found a base large enough to accommodate it, it makes sense to attach it to the base before you begin adding other materials for several reasons. First, this order enables you to arrange other materials around the prop so that it looks like a natural, integral part of the wreath, instead of like some dumb thing someone stuck on top at the last minute. Second, if you wait until last to add the prop, its size and weight will probably damage the smaller, more delicate materials in the wreath.

Design is one of those terrible words that can strike fear in a crafter's heart. A wreath that is well designed, though, is just pleasing to the eye. That's all there is to it. A well-designed wreath can be excruciatingly simple or very complex; the materials can be very expensive or freebies from Mother Nature. As long as you work with attractive materials, the circle shape of the wreath base will help ensure a beautiful finished wreath. The pages that follow should give you several approaches if you're still nervous, although you may find that many of your choices will be dictated by the types and quantities of materials you have available.

Tips of the Trade

• If you're attaching materials to a straw, foam, or moss base with picks or floral pins, be sure to position the materials at an angle, and continue positioning the materials at this same angle all the way around the wreath, rotating the wreath as you work.

• When you're hot-gluing accent materials

to a wreath, arrange them at different depths and angles in the background material.

• Don't be concerned about making the wreath completely symmetrical and perfectly bal-

anced. Some materials, such as fresh flowers, vegetables, and ribbons look better spilling over the confines of the base.

• When using large props or other objects, remember that the visual "weight" of the object may make the wreath look un-balanced. Offset the prop by arranging several small-er materials on the opposite side of the wreath.

Backgrounds and accents, as the name implies, begins with a background material into which accent materials are added. The background material can be a single item, such as a background of Fraser fir for a holiday wreath, or it can be made from several different materials that are the same color. The type of background material you choose will determine the feel of the wreath. A background of the statice known as caspia, for example, will create a delicate, whimsical-looking wreath, whereas a background of something more sturdy, such as pinecones or evergreens, will have a more rustic look.

The best wreath designers choose their accent materials with care. Ideally, these materials should be in a color that contrasts or complements the background color, and since you'll need so few of them, it's worth the trouble to search out something really special. Look for items with intricate detail or special meaning. Accent materials are usually added last to prevent their being damaged by heavier background materials. they are usually attached with hot glue, although floral pins or wire are also options if you're not in a rush.. For best effect, be sure to position the materials at different depths and angles.

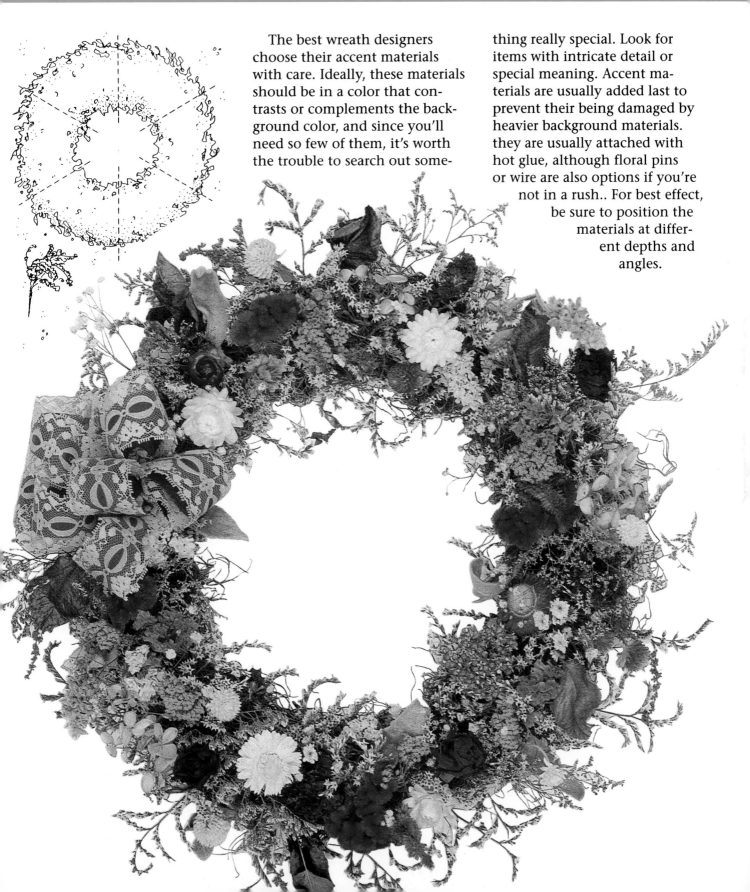

The multiple surface areas of a wreath base can be outlined in different materials for stunning effects. The inner and outer edges of the base can be picked with a simple material such as German statice, leaving the top surface area to be covered with colorful, contrasting materials. The inner and outer edges can also be covered with different colors and varieties of materials, and the top surface area can be subdivided into two or three areas and outlined as well. There are no rules: look closely at your materials and let them dictate your choices.

Another style of wreath making is the hodgepodge design. Success-

ful hodgepodge wreaths appear to have lots of materials attached in random order. Actually, though, the order probably wasn't random at all. To make a hodgepodge design, first sort your materials by size, weight, and delicacy. Arrange the largest and heaviest materials around the base first and secure them in place with wire and/or hot glue. Next, fill in gaps with other materials, taking care to space out different colors and shapes more or less equally around the base. Add the smallest, most delicate materials last, positioning them to showcase their beauty and also to fill in any bare spots. Since there is no single focal point to this type of wreath, you can place the bow anywhere you like.

Materials
Moss-covered straw base, floral pins, glue gun, fresh bay, yarrow, feverfew, anise hyssop, baby's-breath, oregano, roses, sage, crested celosia, horehound, tansy, and violets.

Design Notes
The herbs in this wreath were pinned and hot-glued to the base fresh-cut from the garden. They will dry in place in just a few weeks. If the materials shrink enough to cause bare spots, you can always increase the wreath's fullness with additional clusters of herbs.

Materials
Wire-reinforced foam base, wire cutters, floral wire, glue gun, silk Fraser fir, silk fruit and berries, music ornaments, sheet music, and a large bow.

Design Notes
To make this wreath, first cut the Fraser fir into 7-inch (17 cm) lengths and trim away a few needles at the bottom of each stem to expose the wire. Cover the base by inserting the stems at an angle into the base. Next, wire the bow to the top of the wreath, and finish by hot-gluing the fruit, ornaments, and rolled-up sheet music into the fir.

Materials
Double-wire ring base, floral wire, glue gun, paper ribbon, pinecones (whole and cut into flowers), assorted nuts, sweet gum tree pods, dried German statice, and red clover.

Design Notes
Create a flat surface area on the base by wrapping the unraveled paper ribbon all the way around the double-wire ring. Slip a 6-inch (15 cm) length of floral wire between the bottom petals of each whole pinecone and twist to secure. Then wire the cones to the outer edge of the base by perforating the paper ribbon with the floral wire and twist-ing to secure. Then arrange the remaining materials around the base and hot-glue them in place.

Materials
Vine base, glue gun, fresh silver dollar eucalyptus, acacia, saf-flower, wood mushrooms, moss, pin cushion protea, and grapes.

Design Notes
Fresh grapes add a natural energy to this wreath, and they can be removed and replaced as needed. All of the other materials can be hot-glued in place when fresh and left to dry in place. Leaving most of the vine base undecorated allows the base to become an integral part of the design.

Materials
Straw base, floral picks, glue gun, dried German statice, baby's-breath, peppergrass, annual statice, paper flowers, and satin ribbon.

Design Notes
A solid background of German statice was first picked into the base. Next, the satin ribbon was loosely wrapped around the wreath in even intervals and hot-glued in place as needed. Last, the flowers were hot-glued into the statice. The similar colorings of the dried flowers was achieved by purchasing commercially dyed materials.

Materials
Double-wire metal ring base, glue gun, large dried peppers, miniature corn, pinecone flowers, seedpods, eucalyptus, and a raffia bow.

Design Notes
Wrapping a large double-wire metal ring base with brown paper shipping tape created a wide, flat surface area for the peppers. The peppers were hot-glued in place at various angles, and the remaining materials were hot-glued on next to add visual interest and fill bare spots. The natural raffia bow provides the perfect finishing touch.

Materials
Foam base, wide and narrow ribbon, floral pins and wire, glue gun, silk foliage and flowers, and antique boots.

Design Notes
This variation of the traditional wreath can be created with just about any prop. The boots were attached to the wreath's base with floral pins (inserted through the lace openings) and heavy-gauge wire. After the boots were attached, the bow was attached to the top of the wreath. Last, sprigs of silk foliage and flowers were hot-glued under the bow and boots, and short lengths of narrow ribbon curls were attached with floral pins.

Materials
Twig base spray painted white, glue gun, small pieces of driftwood, moss, paper succulents, and wild vines.

Design Notes
The success of this table centerpiece wreath can be attributed to the designer's respect for the non-conforming nature of the materials. The driftwood pieces were first hot-glued to the base. Next, the succulents were arranged and hot-glued. Small pieces of moss were then hot-glued around the driftwood, and lengths of wild vine were loosely wrapped around the wreath.

Cusick, Dawn, and Pulleyn, Rob. *Wreaths 'Round the Year*. New York: Sterling Publishing Co., 1990.

Pulleyn, Rob. *The Wreath Book*. New York: Sterling Publishing Co., 1988.

Taylor, Carol. *Herbal Wreaths*. New York: Sterling Publishing Co., 1992.

Index